HAPPINESS

in your pocket

ANNA BARNES

HAPPINESS IN YOUR POCKET

This edition copyright © Summersdale Publishers Ltd, 2021
First published in 2016 as *How to Be Happy*

Design by Luci Ward

Research by Anna Martin

An Hachette UK Company
www.hachette.co.uk

Vie Books, an imprint of Summersdale Publishers Ltd
Part of Octopus Publishing Group Limited
Carmelite House
50 Victoria Embankment
LONDON
EC4Y 0DZ
UK

www.summersdale.com

Printed and bound in China

ISBN: 978-1-78783-662-4

Substantial discounts on bulk quantities of Summersdale books are available to corporations, professional associations and other organizations. For details contact general enquiries: telephone: +44 (0) 1243 771107 or email: enquiries@summersdale.com.

Contents

Introduction...4

Techniques for Being Happy..........................6

Sharing Joy...48

Happiness in the Home.............................69

Sleep Well, Feel Well..................................88

Happiness at Work......................................99

Eating for Joy..116

Exercise Your Way to Happiness...........134

Treatments and Therapies for a Happier You....146

INTRODUCTION

With the rapid pace of modern life, and the ever-increasing demands on us to be better, have more and work harder, we often forget about our mental well-being and how important it is to be happy. This book encourages you to take a step back and be more mindful of the different aspects of your life, offering ways to boost your mood and achieve long-lasting happiness, from improving your home environment to managing stressful situations at work, as well as easy-to-follow tips on thinking positively and being proactive about maintaining a healthy body and mind. With a bit of enthusiasm and dedication, these tips will start you on the path to a new, happier you.

Techniques for Being Happy

By picking up this book
you've made a positive
start in your bid for lasting
happiness. Within these
pages you'll find tips to
bring more harmony and
happiness into your life by
adjusting your lifestyle and
mindset, along with simple
techniques to allay negative
thoughts and anxieties by
relaxing your body and mind.

Happiness, not in another place but this place, not for another hour but this hour.

Walt Whitman

find your

own path to

Happiness

and follow it.

CHOOSING TO BE HAPPY

Happiness is not "one size fits all", and there are many reasons why people struggle to stay happy and positive. William James, a prominent American psychologist in the nineteenth century, studied why some people are naturally happy while others struggle. Having suffered from depression he had many insights about the pursuit of happiness and believed ultimately that we choose to be happy; that the act of believing that you can be happy will in turn lead to your happiness. So the next time you feel low, think back to a time when you were happy and immerse yourself in those happy thoughts and believe that you can attain that level of happiness again.

happiness

is by choice,
not by chance.

THE BEST THINGS IN LIFE ARE FREE!

Research has shown that simple experiences like dipping your toes in the sea or having a cup of tea in the sunshine afford far greater pleasure than attaining material goods, so rather than hitting the shops for retail therapy when you need a happiness hit, head outside for some free mood-lifting entertainment!

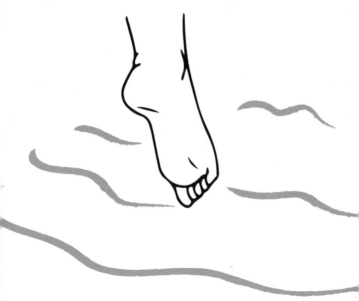

A

MULTITUDE

OF

SMALL DELIGHTS

CONSTITUTE

HAPPINESS.

Charles Baudelaire

TALK IT OUT

Talking to a good friend (or friends) about your problems helps you to put your own worries in perspective, and conversely congratulating each other on the good things happening in your lives is a wonderful way to boost your happiness levels. When you're stuck in a negative spiral, talk to people who can put things into perspective and offer solutions, and if they can make you laugh at the same time, even better.

Never apologize for being you.

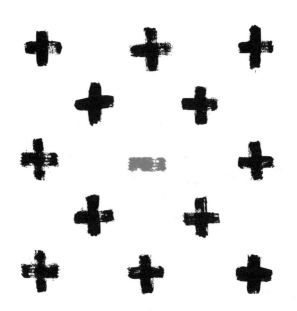

DON'T LET ANYONE
MAKE YOU FEEL BAD

It's important to recognize the people in your life who feed your negative thinking, or belittle you. Don't feel obliged to spend time with them – life is too short to waste time on people who don't have your best interests at heart.

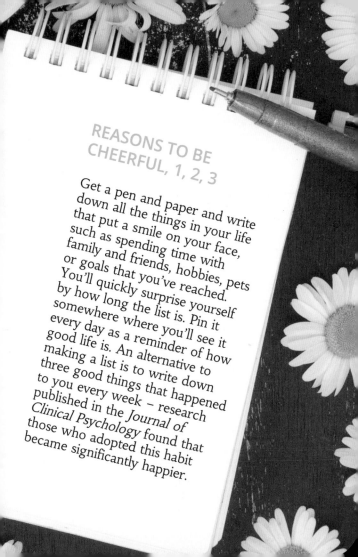

REASONS TO BE CHEERFUL, 1, 2, 3

Get a pen and paper and write down all the things in your life that put a smile on your face, such as spending time with family and friends, hobbies, pets or goals that you've reached. You'll quickly surprise yourself by how long the list is. Pin it somewhere where you'll see it every day as a reminder of how good life is. An alternative to making a list is to write down three good things that happened to you every week – research published in the *Journal of Clinical Psychology* found that those who adopted this habit became significantly happier.

One of the best
ways to make
yourself happy
in the present
is to reminisce
on happy times
from your past.

GIVE YOURSELF A GOAL OR INTENTION FOR THE DAY BEFORE GETTING UP

It could be something as simple as "stay calm at work" or "be more productive" or "enjoy working with my colleagues", but don't make it an actual "thing" to do as this could cause anxiety. The Dalai Lama once said, "Every day, think as you wake up: today I am fortunate to be alive, I have a precious human life, I am not going to waste it." Hold this thought to remind yourself that every day is special and cannot be lived again.

One positive thought in the morning can change your whole day.

Do not spoil what you have by
desiring what you have not;
but remember that what you
now have was once among
the things only hoped for.

Epicurus

MAKE A MOOD BOARD

Mood boards aren't just for those who make art and interiors. A mood board can help you to stay focused on attaining your goals, and keep your mood buoyant. Start by gathering together beautiful images of places you want to visit, zingy colours and fabric swatches, and inspiring quotes and snippets of poetry that make you smile every time you read them. Hang your mood board in a prominent place and keep adding to it as your goals and dreams evolve.

Very little is needed to
make a happy life; it is
all within yourself, in
your way of thinking.

Marcus Aurelius

MAKE
TIME FOR
YOURSELF

It's very easy to forget
your own needs when
you lead a busy life
full of responsibilities.
Allocate time to yourself
on a regular basis –
even blocking out time
on your calendar as "me
time" – to just do the
things that you enjoy
or to sit and think or
meditate and appreciate
your own company.

ENJOY A TREAT
EVERY DAY

If you're feeling sad, tense or anxious, try doing something nice – however small – every day to give yourself a happiness boost. Whether it's making a sumptuous dessert to have with your dinner, going to bed early to read a book, enjoying a long soak in the bath or meeting a friend for coffee, having something to look forward to will help you remain positive throughout the day. Look through your diary and make sure you have treats booked in at regular intervals to keep you happy. The treats don't even need to cost any money – if it's sunny, head out to the park with a friend and take some tennis rackets and a ball; if it's cold, look for free events in your local area or visit a friend.

SMILE AND THE WORLD WILL SMILE BACK.

SMILE!

Smiling releases endorphins, the body's natural feel-good drug. Even if you don't feel like it, turning up the corners of your mouth into a smile will boost your mood. Recent studies have shown that through the enhancement of positive emotions with facial expressions, a person's mood begins to align with the emotion that their face is communicating, so show those pearly whites! It's also worth remembering the old adage that it takes fewer muscles to smile than frown.

If you walk in joy,
happiness is close behind.

Todd Stocker

KEEP CHALLENGING YOURSELF

It may take years of patience and graft to master a skill, such as drawing well or learning a foreign language, but studies show that you have a greater chance of being happier day-to-day in the long term if you actively pursue a pastime or course of study. That feeling of losing yourself in study or a creative pursuit is referred to as "flow", and this state, according to some psychologists, is where true happiness lies.

Choose a job you love,
and you will never have to
work a day in your life.

Confucius

STEER YOUR LIFE TO HAPPINESS

Do you know what you want from your life? Are you happy in your work? What about your personal life? If your current situation is making you unhappy then it's time to make some changes. What could you change that might make you feel more positive? Set realistic goals that help you feel inspired and excited about making changes – and choose the goals that are right for you, not ones to please anyone else. First, write down your aspirations and try to adopt a realistic plan for achieving them. If you fancy a career change, why not take the first step by seeing a careers advisor or getting work experience in your chosen field? Tell yourself that by this time next year you'll be well on the way to making positive changes in your life.

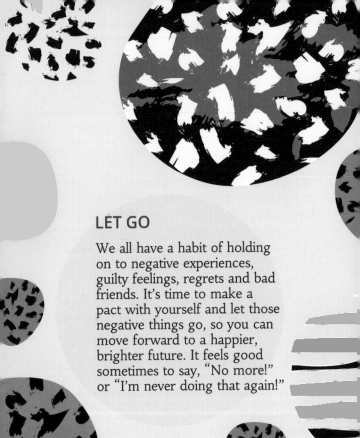

LET GO

We all have a habit of holding on to negative experiences, guilty feelings, regrets and bad friends. It's time to make a pact with yourself and let those negative things go, so you can move forward to a happier, brighter future. It feels good sometimes to say, "No more!" or "I'm never doing that again!"

Whatever has
gone before,
you can always
take a fresh
step into a
hopeful future.

BE YOU

Revel in what makes you different and follow your own path to happiness. Don't feel under pressure to do or be what others expect of you – because no one knows you better than you know yourself.

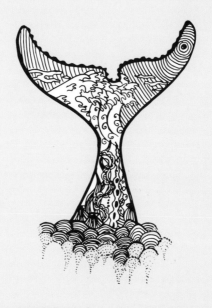

Happiness is essentially a
state of going somewhere,
wholeheartedly, one-directionally,
without regret or reservation.

William Herbert Sheldon

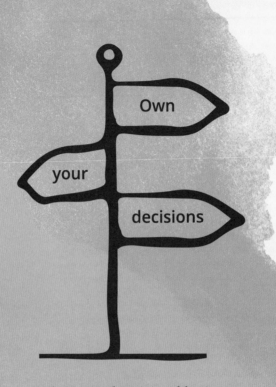

Own

your

decisions

Sticking to a decision and having the courage of your convictions is a sure route to true happiness, because it makes you feel in control of your life and the master (or mistress) of your own destiny.

Always be a
first-rate version
of yourself,
instead of a
second-rate
version of
somebody else.

Judy Garland

**DON'T COMPARE
YOURSELF TO OTHERS**

Continually striving for perfection, which in itself is an impossible goal, will prevent you from being happy and deny you the opportunity to feel good about all that you are achieving or have achieved. One of the most common traits of a perfectionist is to compare yourself with others, such as considering someone else to have a better job, a bigger house, more money, etc. than you, which steers you away from looking at all the positive things happening in your life. Don't believe that emulating others will make you happy; try to be the best version of you and look at the areas in your life that could be improved upon as well as recognizing and appreciating what you're good at.

**REPEAT THIS
MANTRA:**

**I AM
RESPONSIBLE
FOR MY OWN
HAPPINESS.**

I AM
RESPONSIBLE
FOR MY OWN
HAPPINESS. I AM
RESPONSIBLE
FOR MY OWN
I AM HAPPINESS.
RESPONSIBLE
FOR MY OWN
HAPPINESS. I AM
RESPONSIBLE
FOR MY OWN
HAPPINESS.

VISUALIZE A
HAPPIER YOU

When starting out on your journey to lasting happiness, it can be hard to see what the end result will be. It is easy to be put off by "what if"s a situation might bring to mind, and this is where creative visualization can help. Find a comfortable chair to sit in and relax. Begin by closing your eyes and focusing on the natural rhythm of your breathing. Next, start to build up a picture in your head of how a happier, more content you, would look and behave. Where are you? Who is beside you in this happy place? Notice every detail and enjoy how it feels. While you are working on becoming happier with your life, carry this mental image with you as inspiration.

SHARING JOY

An act to make
another happy
inspires the other to
make still another
happy, and so
happiness is aroused
and abounds.

Buddha

THE GIFT OF GIVING

Doing things for others is not only a great way to take your mind off problems; it also feels good. One recent study concluded that those who volunteer for selfless reasons live longer, and altruism is also linked to stronger and happier relationships. There are many ways that you can volunteer your free time, such as helping out at a local charity. Closer to home, consider visiting someone you know who doesn't have family nearby and would appreciate some company, or offer to do the supermarket shop for an elderly neighbour.

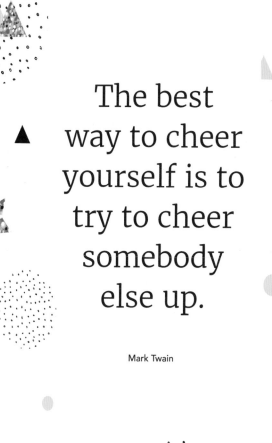

The best
way to cheer
yourself is to
try to cheer
somebody
else up.

Mark Twain

BE GENEROUS

According to research,
money can buy happiness,
but only if you spend it
on someone other than
yourself. It's a win–win,
because not only will you
make someone else feel
special but by doing so, you'll
make yourself happy too!

A JOY AIRED IS A JOY SHARED.

BOOK AN EXPERIENCE OR HOLIDAY WITH FRIENDS

Think about holidays or days out that you've spent with friends and the stories that you still talk about relating to these trips when you get together. Shared experiences are proven to offer greater, longer-lasting happiness, as the experiences can be reminisced about for years to come – the things that go wrong often provide the funniest memories! And it's not just the enjoyment of the experience and the ability to reminisce about it; it's also the planning and anticipation that makes us feel positive and happy. As if you needed any excuse to start researching that next trip!

Friends are the artists who
paint happy lips on your face.

Richelle E. Goodrich

ORGANIZE A
MOVIE NIGHT

Host a movie night
for a group of
friends. Pick your
favourite comedy
to ensure plenty of
laughs and don't
forget the popcorn!

WRITE A LETTER

Most of us have relatives or friends who live at the other end of the country, or have even emigrated. Give yourself (and them) a boost by sitting down to write a letter by hand, letting them know what you've been up to and asking them plenty of questions. Use this as an opportunity to catch up in a way you wouldn't be able to over the phone or via Facebook, by being honest and open, and perhaps sending a little memento such as a photograph along with your note. You will most likely get a handwritten reply, too, which will add to the sense of joy and satisfaction.

SING FOR JOY

Singing provides a wonderful happiness boost and it's a great stress reliever too – it's hard to sing and feel stressed at the same time! It's also good for your health as it releases "feel good" endorphins and the deep breathing required increases oxygen levels in the blood. Another positive aspect of singing is that it improves posture and tones your tummy. Singing in a choir or singing group is even more rewarding as it's a great way to make friends and have fun at the same time – see www. naturalvoice.net for choirs in your locale.

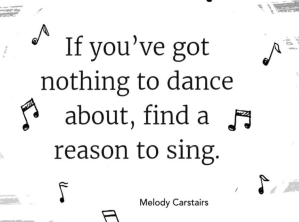

If you've got
nothing to dance
about, find a
reason to sing.

Melody Carstairs

Sending a thoughtful card, email or gift on someone's birthday means you'll be in touch with the people that matter most at least once a year – a good start for building and maintaining important relationships.

GIVE SOMEONE A HUG

A good hug is one of the quickest ways to boost happiness levels as it encourages the flow of oxytocin, which soothes your nervous system, lowering blood pressure and stress levels.

GIVE COMPLIMENTS

Giving or receiving a heartfelt compliment boosts self-esteem and happiness levels – so make the effort to make someone's day. Tell them how great they look, how much you like and admire something about them (e.g. a personality trait), or if a work colleague has submitted an impressive report thank them sincerely – chances are you'll receive a compliment back. Be sure to thank someone when they have given you a compliment and take a moment to truly enjoy what has been said. In the same way, save complimentary emails, cards and messages, and file away your best performance reviews at work. Re-read these words whenever you need a boost.

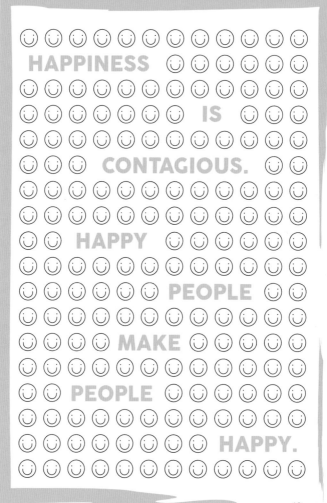

HAPPINESS IS CONTAGIOUS. HAPPY PEOPLE MAKE PEOPLE HAPPY.

When was the last time you told someone you loved them? "I love you" is so powerful, and to say it to a family member, a partner or a close friend will mean the world to them – and when they reciprocate, it will mean the world to you too!

The happiness of life is made up of
minute fractions – the little, soon
forgotten charities of a kiss or smile,
a kind look, a heartfelt compliment,
and the countless infinitesimals of
pleasurable and genial feeling.

Samuel Taylor Coleridge

MAKE A PHONE CALL

Call up one person a day for a catch-up or a gossip – studies show that even if we're having an off day, speaking to a loved one will make us feel happier.

WALK A DOG FOR A FRIEND OR FAMILY MEMBER

Offering to walk someone's dog frees up time for them to do more for themselves, while giving you the opportunity to get out into nature and share that with an animal companion. Dog walking is a positive experience for both you and the pet; not only does it offer the chance for some green exercise for both you and the dog, but it is well known that spending time with animals provides a mood boost.

Nothing can
make our life,
or the lives of
other people,
more beautiful
than perpetual
kindness.

Leo Tolstoy

HAPPINESS IN THE HOME

Home should be the one place where you feel happiest and most relaxed. If you find that it has become a source of stress, the following tips will help you to turn your home back into a place of joy, comfort and calm.

When you love
what you have, you
have everything
you need.

CLEAR THE CLUTTER

Having a tidy, clutter-free home is important for general happiness and well-being. Think about that time when you were late for work because you couldn't find your car keys, or when you spent ages looking for a particular outfit because your cupboard was too full – it doesn't set the day off to a good start and can leave you feeling overwhelmed and upset. Having clear surfaces and a place for everything is calming, and the act of tidying can be satisfying too; the low-impact workout that comes from sorting and cleaning produces serotonin, the hormone that balances mood and makes us happy.

REPEAT THIS MANTRA:

I DESERVE HAPPINESS
I DESERVE HAPPINESS
I DESERVE HAPPINESS
I DESERVE HAPPINESS
I DESERVE HAPPINESS
I DESERVE HAPPINESS
I DESERVE HAPPINESS
I DESERVE HAPPINESS

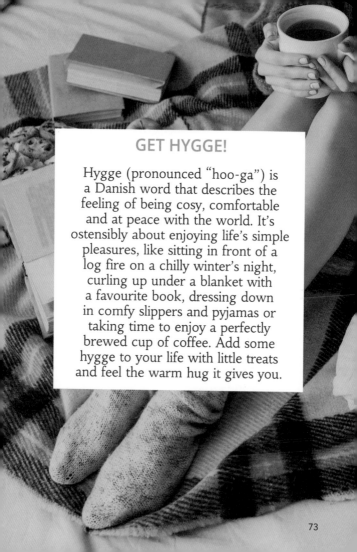

GET HYGGE!

Hygge (pronounced "hoo-ga") is a Danish word that describes the feeling of being cosy, comfortable and at peace with the world. It's ostensibly about enjoying life's simple pleasures, like sitting in front of a log fire on a chilly winter's night, curling up under a blanket with a favourite book, dressing down in comfy slippers and pyjamas or taking time to enjoy a perfectly brewed cup of coffee. Add some hygge to your life with little treats and feel the warm hug it gives you.

SORT OUT YOUR WARDROBE

We accumulate so many clothes over the years, but it can be surprisingly hard to let go of the things that we no longer wear. Whether it's the belief that we will slim down into that favourite old pair of jeans, or having a sentimental attachment to something, many of us have wardrobes and drawers that are stuffed to the gills. The way to clear out the things you no longer need is to ask yourself these questions honestly as you're sorting through:

1. Do I love it?

2. Do I ever wear it?

3. Do I want to be seen out in this?

4. Is it itchy or uncomfortable to wear?

Once you've bagged up all the items that you're never going to wear again, sort through things that you might want to sell online and take the rest to a charity shop. Give the clothes that you're keeping due respect and purchase some good hangers. When it comes to filling the drawers, roll your items to avoid creases, and stand them up in the drawer so you can see all your items at once. Soon, simply opening your wardrobe or pulling open a drawer will bring a smile to your face every morning. Don't stop there, though – tackle the linen cupboard, the kitchen cabinets and your handbag too, to truly enjoy being happily clutter-free!

The true secret of happiness lies in taking a genuine interest in all the details of daily life.

William Morris

DON'T TAKE YOURSELF TOO SERIOUSLY

- LEARN TO LAUGH AT YOURSELF.

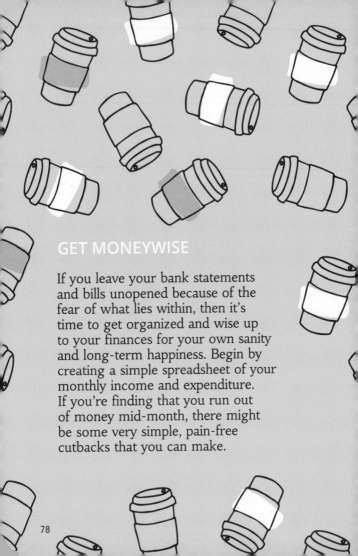

GET MONEYWISE

If you leave your bank statements
and bills unopened because of the
fear of what lies within, then it's
time to get organized and wise up
to your finances for your own sanity
and long-term happiness. Begin by
creating a simple spreadsheet of your
monthly income and expenditure.
If you're finding that you run out
of money mid-month, there might
be some very simple, pain-free
cutbacks that you can make.

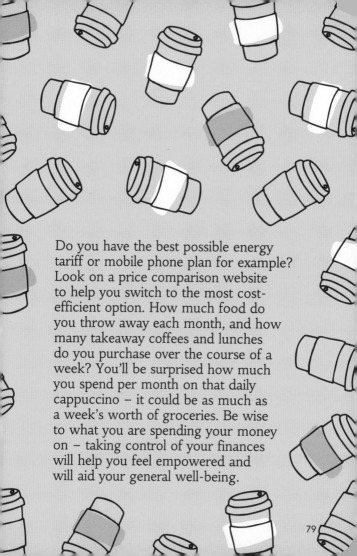

Do you have the best possible energy tariff or mobile phone plan for example? Look on a price comparison website to help you switch to the most cost-efficient option. How much food do you throw away each month, and how many takeaway coffees and lunches do you purchase over the course of a week? You'll be surprised how much you spend per month on that daily cappuccino – it could be as much as a week's worth of groceries. Be wise to what you are spending your money on – taking control of your finances will help you feel empowered and will aid your general well-being.

LEARN TO UNPLUG

It's the easiest thing to come home after a day at work and sit in front of the TV, regardless of whether there is something you actually want to watch or not, or go online and lose yourself in social media. Before you know it, hours have passed and the evening is over. Shake up your routine and rather than reaching for the remote, tablet or smartphone, make time for hobbies you love, invite friends round or go on a date night with your partner – you'll soon feel excited about coming home with so many things to look forward to.

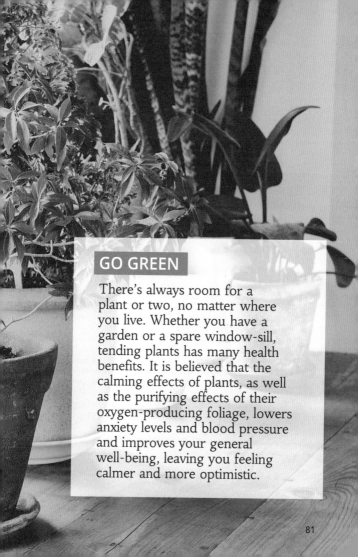

GO GREEN

There's always room for a plant or two, no matter where you live. Whether you have a garden or a spare window-sill, tending plants has many health benefits. It is believed that the calming effects of plants, as well as the purifying effects of their oxygen-producing foliage, lowers anxiety levels and blood pressure and improves your general well-being, leaving you feeling calmer and more optimistic.

Nothing
great was ever
achieved without
enthusiasm.

Ralph Waldo Emerson

LEARN TO LOVE CLEANING!

There are certain jobs that you just can't get out of, such as doing the dishes or cleaning the bathroom, so learn to love them – or at least pretend to! Put some music on and sing at the top of your voice. Do some fist pumps at the chorus and whoop at every small victory! Studies have shown that listening to music while doing chores makes you feel positive and happy, and makes the job less arduous.

GET A FURRY FRIEND

A recent survey found that pet owners generally enjoyed greater levels of self-esteem and significantly lower levels of stress and depression than those without pets. Pets provide a sense of meaning and belonging, and they're also great fun because they love to play and interact with the world around them.

Happiness
is a warm
puppy.

Charles M. Schulz

MAKE TIME FOR PLAY

Do something silly
just for fun – kick up
leaves, build a sandcastle,
tackle the monkey
bars in the park, make
a paper aeroplane...
Challenge yourself to
do something playful
and fun every day.

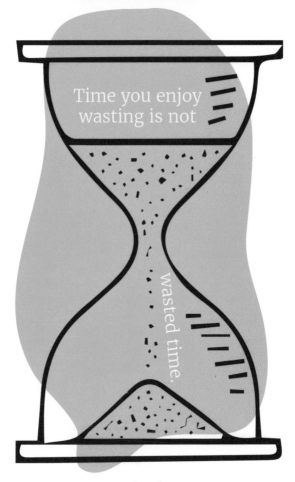

Time you enjoy
wasting is not

wasted time.

Marthe Troly-Curtin

Sleep Well, Feel Well

It's no surprise that being tired is not conducive to happiness. Lack of sleep weakens the immune system, slows reaction times and makes us more prone to depression, anxiety and low mood. Seven hours' sleep a night is generally regarded as the minimum amount required in order to remain healthy. The following tips will encourage a better night's sleep so that you feel energized and positive at the start of each new day.

LISTEN TO CLASSICAL MUSIC BEFORE BED

Studies have shown that listening to classical music lowers body temperature and heart rate and calms your breathing, which is ideal for inducing a restful night's sleep.

A comfortable home is a great
source of happiness. It ranks
immediately after health
and a good conscience.

Sydney Smith

MAKE YOUR BEDROOM A HAPPY ZONE

Your bedroom should be a sanctuary – a place for sleep and sex only. Keep it devoid of clutter, open the windows for a period each day to allow fresh air to flow through, and regularly change the bedding, to keep it crisp, fresh and inviting. Opt for soft lighting, and try not to have screens in the room – that includes TVs, tablets, laptops and phones – as using these before bedtime makes it difficult to sleep. Only have pictures and knick-knacks that bring you joy. Light some scented candles, such as lavender, chamomile and vanilla, which promote relaxation and restorative sleep.

Only surround yourself with things that bring joy to your heart.

92

Optimism is true
moral courage.

Ernest Shackleton

MAKE YOUR BED

This is one of the simplest of tasks that can make you feel happier. Also, having bedding that suits you and helps you to feel better about yourself and your surroundings can give you a great positivity boost; as well as the benefit to your quality of sleep, attractive linen helps make your bedroom a place you are proud of, and that you feel comfortable and relaxed in. Choosing the right bed linen means choosing something that will make you feel cosy and ready to sleep in the evening, and fresh and ready to go in the morning. For some people, cool cotton sheets and duvet covers work best; others find silk gentler against their skin. For many people, synthetic fabrics make them sweat too much in the night, which can cause night-time waking, leaving you unrefreshed and even jittery. Invest in a couple of sets of good linen, rather than multiple cheap and cheerful sets of polyester sheets, to help you feel more positive about your bedroom.

ADD A SPLASH OF COLOUR

Bright colours are proven to make you feel more positive and happy, so add splashes of colour, like a red throw for the bed, or a picture of a colourful, sunny landscape, to perk you up in the mornings.

CLEAR YOUR MIND BEFORE SLEEP

One of the most common factors of sleep deprivation is worry. It's important to clear your mind of negative thoughts before you go to bed. There are a number of ways to do this, such as writing down what's on your mind or compiling a to-do list for the next day. Another idea is to chat to a friend or loved one, preferably someone who sees the lighter side and will help you to put things into perspective. Thinking of three good things that happened to you in the day is also a great way to banish negative thoughts and go to bed with a positive frame of mind.

TAKE
TIME
TO DO
WHAT
MAKES
YOUR
SOUL
HAPPY.

HAPPINESS AT WORK

On the whole, most of us spend more of our waking hours at work than we do at home. With this in mind, it's especially important to be happy at work. The following tips offer ways to stay positive in your workplace.

MAKE FRIENDS AT WORK

Having a workmate to chat to by the water cooler or to go out to lunch with can make your working day much happier, and more fun! You could start by suggesting a group of you go out for lunch or to the cinema every so often so that you can get to know your colleagues and form lasting friendships.

Associate with people who
are likely to improve you.

Seneca

T H A

N K

SAY
"THANK YOU"

Take the time to
thank people when
they have done a job
well – it will brighten
someone's day and
spread a happy vibe
around the office.

Y O U

DON'T MULTITASK

It's a common misconception that those with a busy roster of jobs need to multitask in order to meet deadlines. According to research multitasking wastes more time than it saves, and it is destructive to a person's creativity and concentration levels. So, instead of firefighting when you have a multitude of jobs, create a list of priorities and focus on one job at a time.

AVOID SECOND-HAND STRESS FROM COLLEAGUES

For many, work is the most stressful aspect of our lives, and when a work colleague is strained you can unconsciously absorb their negativity. One way to avoid this is to try to offer some positive advice when a colleague is talking about their problems. If you find that their behaviour is having a negative impact on your mood, it's often best to take yourself out of the situation and perhaps go and prepare yourself a drink. Be mindful that you have made a choice to be positive and happy, and that you will not adopt your colleague's negative mindset.

KEEP CALM AND STAY POSITIVE

HAVE SOME
HEALTHY SNACKS
ON YOUR DESK

When you are in need of an extra shot of energy at work, it can be tempting to reach for unhealthy sugary snacks, but after the initial sugar rush is over you can start to feel low and sluggish. Instead, treat yourself to some healthy snack options, such as fresh fruit, nuts, popcorn or a small amount of dark chocolate, which will help maintain energy levels and a healthy mind and body.

STRETCH

Sitting down all day and working at a computer can lead to health complaints, such as carpal tunnel syndrome, eye strain, headaches, weight gain and low mood. Try to stretch every so often, or if you're on a short break, run up and down stairs or get outside and take a short walk. The endorphins released will give you a positive energy boost and you'll feel better able to cope with the daily demands of your job.

WITH EVERY JOB THAT MUST BE DONE THERE SHOULD BE AN ELEMENT OF FUN!

Everyone has aspects of their job that they don't enjoy, and that they have to grit their teeth to get done. Try to approach these jobs with an element of fun. If you're doing filing, for example, make up word games and riddles using people's surnames, or if you have a large document to read through, try making a rubber-band ball at the same time, which can latterly be used as a stress reliever.

There is no duty we so much underrate as the duty of being happy.

Robert Louis Stevenson

LEARN TO SAY "NO"

This applies to all aspects of life, but it's something we come across most often at work when demands are made of us and we don't feel we can say "no" because it might reflect badly on us. The concept of saying "no" to your superior when they ask you to complete a task can be a daunting one, but it is important not to worry that you will lose respect if you refuse. Those in charge understand that sometimes our workload does not permit us to take on additional tasks and responsibilities; they rely on their employees to let them know when and if they are able to do more.

Politely declining a task with the explanation that you will not be able to complete it in the time needed will not only show your boss that you are aware of your workload and limits, it will also help alleviate your stress. If you always feel you have to say "yes" then you may be left with too much work, and will have the added pressure of finishing tasks late, of not completing them to the desired quality, or of having to work additional hours to complete them. This is easy to avoid: just keep an awareness of what you need to do, and say "no" if you need to.

Happiness is a journey, not a destination.

Proverb

KEEP YOUR DESK (AND DESKTOP) TIDY

It's important to keep your desk tidy and have a place for everything, so that you can get on with your job without the stress of constantly trying to find misplaced documents or stationery items. This also rings true with your desktop – don't populate it with old files or pictures; get rid of them! The same goes for old emails and Word documents – delete the ones that you don't need and store the important ones in labelled folders, or archive them.

TAKE A BREAK

It's important to take your holiday entitlement. Everyone needs time away to de-stress and recharge. Taking a break is proven to make us healthier in general and more productive in the workplace, so don't feel guilty about booking those two weeks off!

Happiness
depends upon
ourselves.

Aristotle

EATING FOR JOY

If you could do with a dash of optimism or want to pep up your positivity, then choosing the right foods is an important step towards lasting happiness. Foods rich in minerals, vitamins and fatty acids are not only good for you but they have also been shown to lessen symptoms of depression and anxiety. Studies in how the food we consume affects mood have concluded that there are ten key nutrients that combat low mood and make us feel good.

THESE ARE:

CALCIUM, CHROMIUM,
FOLATE, IRON, MAGNESIUM,
OMEGA-3 FATTY ACIDS,
VITAMIN B6, VITAMIN B12,
VITAMIN D AND ZINC.

The following tips will
help you to achieve
a healthy, balanced
diet that will improve
your happiness levels
from the inside out.

MAX YOUR MINERALS

Minerals are essential for a healthy nervous system, so to ensure general physical and mental well-being, it's important to include them in your diet.

CALCIUM maintains healthy blood vessels and strong bones – low levels of calcium are linked to low mood, particularly in women. Calcium is found in dairy products as well as kale and collard greens.

CHROMIUM is vital for regulating insulin in the body and it also helps the brain to regulate moods, the lack of it leading to an increased risk of high blood pressure and depression. Chromium can be found in broccoli, turkey, potatoes and wholegrain products.

MAGNESIUM plays an important role in the body's production of serotonin, without which there is the risk of a predisposition to stress and irritability. Magnesium is present in nuts, dark, leafy vegetables, fish and wholegrain products.

ZINC is a great mood balancer and is known to reduce symptoms of depression. It can be found in seafood, eggs, beans, mushrooms, nuts, seeds and kiwi fruit.

IRON transports oxygen around the body and strengthens muscle. Depleted levels lead to fatigue, low mood and depression. Iron deficiency is more common in women, and vegetarians might want to consider taking a supplement; find iron in dark-green leafy vegetables, meat, fish, beans, pulses, nuts and wholegrain products.

you can be happy —just believe it.

Happiness comes from within.

KEEP YOUR GI LOW

A low-GI diet can have many health benefits – more steady energy levels, less bloating, no sugar cravings – all of which can help you to stay feeling positive. GI stands for glycaemic index: the ranking of carbohydrate-containing foods based on their overall effect on blood glucose levels. When we eat foods with a high GI, such as white bread, pastries and sweets, our blood sugar spikes and then rapidly drops, leaving us tired, irritable and hungry. Eating low-GI foods – such as beans, rye bread and most fruit and veg – helps ensure your body is fuelled throughout the day and night, avoiding the spikes and dips in your blood sugar that can have a detrimental effect on your emotions, and therefore leaves you feeling more balanced.

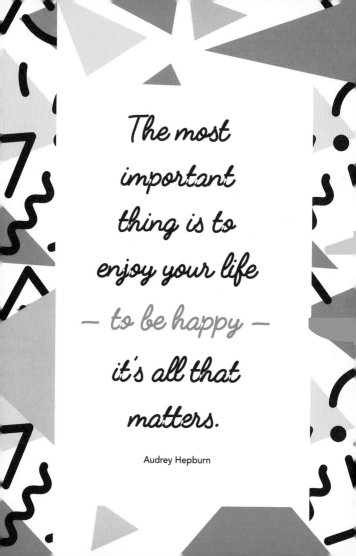

The most important thing is to enjoy your life — to be happy — it's all that matters.

Audrey Hepburn

GO NUTS

Eating two Brazil nuts a day will give you your daily dose of selenium, which is vital for healthy thyroid function. This will improve your mood and significantly decrease anxiety levels.

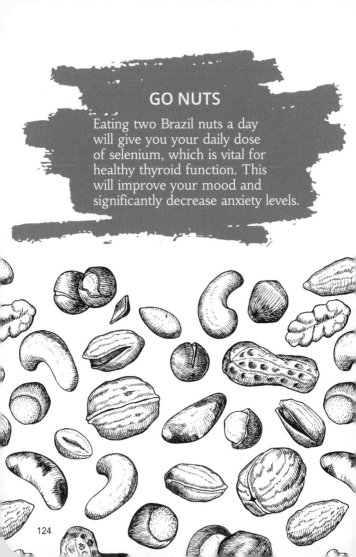

DRINK WATER

Drinking six to eight glasses of water a day is important for mental health, well-being and happiness. This is because water carries nutrients to our body's cells and flushes the toxins out. Dehydration leads to confusion and irritability. Don't forget that hot drinks, fruit juices and fresh food (especially vegetables) also contain water, and so count towards your recommended daily intake.

Eat for Health and long-lasting happiness.

CUT OUT CAFFEINE

If you're prone to anxiety and low mood, it's advisable to cut caffeine from your diet. Some scientists believe that caffeine is the single most important cause of anxiety and that more than nine cups of coffee a day can cause extreme stress and panic attacks. This is because caffeine inhibits the body's receptors of adenosine – a natural sedative that keeps us calm – leaving us feeling overstimulated.

MOODS AND BOOZE

After a long day at the office many people reach for a glass of wine to help them unwind and de-stress. Alcohol is widely known to have a calming effect, as it releases endorphins (the body's natural feel-good drug), but this is negated by the depressant qualities of alcohol and the feeling of anxiety that can be left behind once the effects wear off. Try to cut down on alcohol in general, but if you do fancy a tipple, opt for a glass of Chianti, Merlot or Cabernet Sauvignon, as the grape skins used in these wines are rich in the sleep hormone melatonin.

Optimism is the faith that leads to achievement; nothing can be done without hope.

Helen Keller

GET HAPPY WITH WHOLEGRAINS

While it can be tempting to reach for a slice of cake or a biscuit when negativity strikes, it's important to remember that the combination of sugar and refined flour in these foods can be detrimental to health and cause a wide variety of problems. These issues range from skin conditions to serious illnesses such as diabetes, all of which can cause your mood to dip. Instead, try to incorporate more wholegrains into your diet. This can be as simple as switching white bread for wholemeal, white rice for whole rice, or choosing a breakfast cereal that contains wholegrain rice. You could also try some of the many interesting grains available by getting creative with your cooking – why not try using bulgur wheat in a salad, or millet with a tagine? The options are endless.

GET THE RIGHT BALANCE OF EFAS
(essential fatty acids)

Getting the right amount of omega-3 in your diet is important for maintaining a healthy mind and a positive outlook. Simple steps for doing this include eating two portions of oily fish a week, or by sprinkling a tablespoon of seeds (pumpkin and sunflower) onto cereal or salad every day.

NOW IS THE TIME TO BE HAPPY!

BOOST YOUR MOOD WITH MACA

Maca powder is a superfood made from the maca plant, which grows in the Peruvian Andes. It's described by some as "nature's Viagra" due to its energizing qualities. It's particularly good for women who suffer from PMT and low mood, relieving anxiety, depression and general aches and pains. It also regulates the endocrine system: the glands that regulate mood, metabolism, sexual function and sleep patterns. Try it sprinkled onto cereal or added to smoothies or baked goods.

Exercise Your Way to Happiness

Have you ever noticed how good you feel after a swim, a brisk walk or a jog? It's the release of the "happy" chemicals, endorphins and dopamine, and the reduction in the stress hormones cortisol and adrenalin, that makes you feel so good. According to research, just 20 minutes of exercise can boost your mood for up to 12 hours. The following tips will help you get moving and start to feel the mood-boosting benefits of regular exercise.

An aim in life is the only
fortune worth finding;
and it is not to be found
in foreign lands but
in the heart itself.

Robert Louis Stevenson

EXERCISE WITH FRIENDS

If you're struggling to get motivated to do some exercise, try pairing up with a friend to go jogging or have a round of tennis. Alternatively, join a class or team and rediscover sports that you enjoyed at school, such as netball, football or rugby, or try something new and exciting, like trampolining or rock climbing. Exercising with friends or in a group means that you can motivate each other and have fun at the same time.

An early-morning walk is a blessing for the whole day.

Henry David Thoreau

A BREATH OF FRESH AIR

Studies show that people have a happier outlook if they spend time in nature. Breathing in fresh air and feeling the sun on your face is a wonderful quick fix of vitamin D. Inhaling deep breaths clears your lungs and increases the amount of oxygen being transported around your body, which in turn leads to a clearer mind and greater energy. So instead of meeting a friend at a cafe, go for a walk together in the fresh air, or get off the bus at an earlier stop than usual and walk the extra way to enjoy the benefits of being outside. Take your workout outside by riding a bike to work, signing up for yoga in the park, joining a walking or running group or switching to an outdoor swimming pool in the summer.

LET YOUR HAPPINESS

RADIATE LIKE THE SUN.

He who enjoys doing
and enjoys what he
has done is happy.

Johann Wolfgang von Goethe

LISTEN TO MUSIC WHILE YOU EXERCISE

Studies have shown that listening to high-energy music while exercising boosts mood and makes the workout seem easier. Similarly, watching a favourite show while running on a treadmill makes the activity much more pleasant than staring at yourself getting sweaty in the mirror!

PRACTISE YOGA

The ancient practice of yoga is not just
about bending your body, but also about
balancing your mood. Yoga is practised
at your own pace, allowing you to take
time to really understand what your body
can do. The calming effect it has on the
mind and the physical effects of toning and
strengthening the body can help increase
your contentment levels. Most classes will
finish with yogic sleep, or guided meditation,
which can leave you feeling refreshed,
happier and more in touch with yourself. If
you would rather not attend a class, yoga
can be practised at home with the help of
books, DVDs or online demonstrations.

DANCE YOUR WAY
TO HAPPINESS

Dancing is great fun and it's
also a good workout. You could
try a class: jive, jazz, ballroom
and Latin classes are all great
ways to get fit and meet new
people, and fitness fusion
classes such as Zumba are
becoming ever more popular.
Choose a style that suits you
and, above all, enjoy it.

GO WILD

Try wild swimming in a lake or the sea to experience nature while exercising. The health benefits of immersing yourself in cold water include the soothing of aches and pains and relief from depression and anxiety, as well as providing a boost to your immune system and vitality. The endorphin high from wild swimming makes you feel positive and happy, and ready to take on life's challenges.

Think **BIG** dream *BIGGER.*

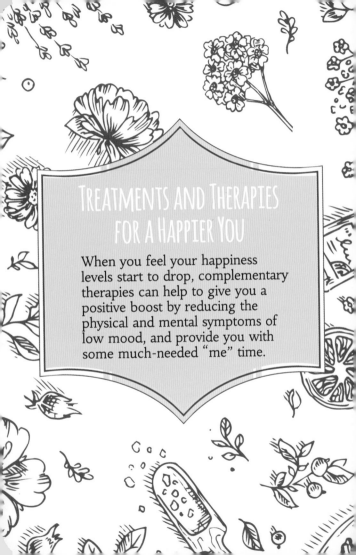

Treatments and Therapies for a Happier You

When you feel your happiness levels start to drop, complementary therapies can help to give you a positive boost by reducing the physical and mental symptoms of low mood, and provide you with some much-needed "me" time.

Now and then it's good to pause in our pursuit of happiness and just be happy.

Guillaume Apollinaire

PRACTISE MEDITATION

Brain scans have shown
that Buddhist monks, who
practise regular meditation,
have happiness levels that
are off the charts. Studies
have shown that those who
meditate for 10 minutes a day
sleep better and are happier
and more resilient when it
comes to handling stress.

The present moment is filled
with joy and happiness. If you
are attentive, you will see it.

Thích Nhất Hạnh

Look in the mirror
and pay yourself
a compliment:

you are
wonderful!

TRY POSITIVITY
MANTRAS

A mantra is a positive phrase that you repeat to yourself. Mantras can be thought quietly to yourself, or said out loud. Many people believe that actually saying your mantra makes it more effective, as vocalizing something gives it more substance. You can also write down your chosen mantra and put it somewhere you are likely to see it, such as the kitchen or bathroom. Choose your mantra based on what is important to you, not what you feel others will accept; it could be anything, from "I will pass my exam" to "I am a good, honest person". Regularly repeating your chosen mantra will help you reaffirm your faith in yourself and your abilities.

Allow happiness in to your life.

HUG A TREE

Connecting to nature is believed to have a significant impact on our well-being and happiness. Try to connect with nature every day and enjoy the positive effects on your health and happiness – it could be something as simple as walking through autumn leaves and listening to the crunching sound they make, stopping to smell a beautiful flower or hugging an ancient oak tree.

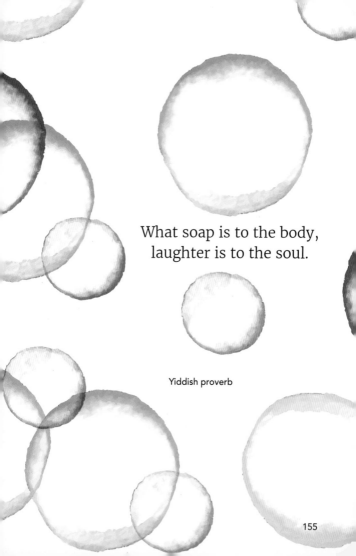

What soap is to the body,
laughter is to the soul.

Yiddish proverb

LAUGHTER IS THE BEST MEDICINE

Laughter is good for you; not only does it release endorphins which make you feel happy, but there are proven health benefits too. A good belly laugh is akin to a mild workout session, because it gets the blood flowing and the muscles working. It also reduces stress hormones and blood pressure as well as giving your immune system a boost, improving memory and having a positive effect on sleep patterns. Here are some tips for adding a little more laughter into your life:

1. Where appropriate, see the funny side of a difficult situation, and try not to take yourself too seriously.

2. Think back to something funny that happened and recount it to a friend – reliving that memory will give your friend a mood boost too!

3. Sign up to daily funny emails or a newsletter from your favourite comedian, and make a habit of regularly reading comic novels and books of jokes or amusing anecdotes.

4. Spend time with people who make you laugh.

5. Watch a funny film or visit a comedy club.

AND FINALLY...
DOCTOR'S ORDERS

If your low mood is having a negative effect on your day-to-day life, it is worth booking an appointment with your doctor to talk about it. Although complementary therapies can help, some situations need medical help. It may be that your doctor recommends a talking therapy such as CBT (cognitive behavioural therapy) or medication to help you. Remember the doctor is there to help, not to judge; tell them everything and that way they will be able to give you the best possible advice.

WE HOPE YOU ENJOY THE JOURNEY TOWARDS A NEW, HAPPIER YOU!

IMAGE CREDITS

If you're interested in finding out more about our books,
find us on Facebook at Summersdale Publishers
and follow us on Twitter at @Summersdale.

WWW.SUMMERSDALE.COM